# SHAKE
## the Atmosphere to Reclaim an Empty Moment

Caroline Reddy

In **Shake the Atmosphere to Reclaim an Empty Moment**, Caroline Reddy embarks on a Zen-inspired journey of self-discovery through woods, labyrinths, and fields of plum blossoms to find "a warrior's heart wrapped in rose scent." Told through a diverse array of poetic styles, the poems in this debut collection travel a galaxy of juxtapositions through universes and micro moments, into the political and the personal, onto roads paved with isolation and ultimately interconnectedness. Take a breath, "anoint [your] wrists with lavender oil," and join the poet as she witnesses the exact moment when "a glass appears/in the kaleidoscope of time," when "a harsh winter settles/into the scent of a new spring moon."

**Claudine Nash** author of
BEGINNER'S GUIDE TO LOSS IN THE MULTIVERSE

With an unflinching slew of brilliant, heart-wrenching poems, Caroline Reddy teaches us what it means to feel, endure, and grow from pain. From her Iranian heritage to her experiences as a healer, Caroline shows us the value of looking at the world with a brave clarity free of illusion. The World needs it, too.

**Tommy Sheffield** author of
THE STRENGTH IT TAKES TO STAY AFLOAT

Caroline Reddy brings a warrior's heart and an explorer's fearlessness to these poems of discovery and reclamation. We travel with her through the hard work required to "rewire a new path" from her childhood in Iran, through the spiritual lessons of her zen and reiki practices, her deep love of the natural world, and up to the celestial spheres in her "steampunk space suit underneath human skin". Infused with wonder and a refusal to accept the world as it is handed to her, these poems are invitation and encouragement to walk "barefoot through the labyrinth" and to join the poet on journeys that will take us beyond ourselves and what we thought we knew into our own star-dusted, limitless possibilities.

**Susan Moorhead** author of THE NIGHT GHOST
and CARRY DARKNESS, CARRY LIGHT

The poems in Caroline Reddy's Shake the Atmosphere to Reclaim an Empty Moment pulse with candor & emotion. In expertly crafted lines, Reddy travels the sprawling trails between trauma & healing, between grief & splendor, often bridging the gap of time— "my childhood blanket / has collected / neuron memories / that can be triggered / any second / by the latest bombs…" This stunning debut catapults an important voice into the literary canon.

**Aldo Amparan** author of
BROTHER SLEEP

Caroline Reddy's collection, Shake the Atmosphere to Reclaim an Empty Moment is a carefully woven tapestry of discovery, ritual, cleansing and strident reckoning of a self with the world that is both harmonious and chaotic. These poems excavate, ask the big questions of life—love, death, loss. Reddy's sonorous voice is evocative and tenderly renders the fleeting and mystical revelations and juxtapositions of nature, war, and identity. A poet with a natural ear for the lyrical, and the careful way sounds and images collide in this collection is a marvel to the senses: "when our soil and soul began to fade/ we trapped a nightingale in a cage." These radiant poems showcase the dualities, the dark and the light, but the poet finds beauty in every breath and we are hanging on every nuance, leaf, and sensation in this soulful, heart staking journey, "as we watch snowflakes /soften underneath the moon/making space for plum blossoms to bloom." Read this collection to burn the brush and find the soul.

**Cynthia Atkins** author of STILL-LIFE WITH GOD
and IN THE EVENT OF FULL DISCLOSURE

Caroline Reddy's use of language and imagery are strong and well carved. Readers enter into experiences that are haunting and unknown. Reading Reddy's poems such as "The Basement of Tehran," & "The Butchering of a Child" in "Shake the Atmosphere to Reclaim an Empty Moment" was powerful, beautiful and painful. Within the unknown lives familiarity, humanity's connection and an unrelenting resiliency.

**Lorraine Currelley**
**New York Beat Poet Laureate** (2023-lifetime)

Copyright © 2024 **Caroline Reddy**
All Rights Reserved

**First Edition, First Printing — March 2024**
Library of Congress Control Number: 2023951429
ISBN 978-1-953136-60-2   Hardback
ISBN 978-1-953136-59-6   Paperback

Cover Design by Kurt Lovelace
Cover Art by Pierian Springs Press
Cover type *Bauhaus Dessau* **Alfarn** by Céline Hurka,
Elia Preuss, Flavia Zimbardi,
Hidetaka Yamasaki, and Luca Pellegrini.
Poetry title and body set in *URW* Baskerville.
Misc. in **Jenson** by Robert Slimbach & **Sabon** by Jan Tschichold.
Flourishes set in Emigre Foundry **Dalliance**, by Frank Heine &
Emigre Foundry **ZeitGuys**, by Bob Aufuldish, Eric Donelan.
Typefaces licensed Adobe, Linotype, & URW GmbH.

PSPress.Pub
Pierian Springs Press, Inc
30 N Gould St, Ste 30
Sheridan, Wyoming 82801

For my madar
Parivash Khandani

# Contents

- The Basement of Tehran ... 2
- The Butchering of a Child ... 5
- Torn ... 6
- An Outburst from a Desperate Soul ... 7
- Homesickness in this Stringent Atmosphere: ... 9
- A Nightingale Reaches a Crescendo ... 10
- Sanctity of the Muses ... 11
- Plum Blossom (Baika) ... 12
- At The Temple of Konohanasakuya-hime ... 13
- The Final Dokusan (My Zen Teacher's Last Breath) ... 15
- The Retreat ... 17
- The Compassion of Kami ... 19
- The Dome of the Fireflies ... 21
- Ensō: The Hand Drawn Brushstrokes ... 23
- Four Haikus ... 24
- Particles of Light ... 25
- Pods ... 26
- Amidst the Grip of Abandonment and Comfort ... 27
- A Sacred Dance ... 29
- The Lion's Gate ... 30
- The Lost Tribe ... 31
- Krishna's Cart ... 33
- The Lighthouse ... 35
- The Phoenicia Moon ... 36

| | |
|---|---|
| Surrender | 37 |
| Winter Clothes | 39 |
| Spellcaster | 41 |
| Star Being | 42 |
| A Star Being's Chronicle | 43 |
| Sorry that My Earthquake was so Profound | 46 |
| We've Brought Apocalypse Through the Walls | 47 |
| Mosaics of the Warrior Spirit | 48 |
| When whales Carry our Destiny | 49 |
| A conversation with Sophia's Universe | 50 |
| The Taboo of the Hand | 51 |
| Generation X Marks the Spot | 54 |
| A Warrior's Heart | 55 |

 Publications   57-58

 Acknowledgments   59

 About the Author   60

# SHAKE the Atmosphere to Reclaim an Empty Moment

# The Basement of Tehran

Hold still child
to that fuzzy blanket
until the siren stops

And
when bombs
drop:

we have this space

beneath us

that holds still
as we take shelter

Underneath

the loud alarm.

When fear reigns
stop:

*Azizam:*

smell fresh
Nivea scent of your mother's hand;
pull closer to your *madar.*

I tug at my *papush:*

my childhood blanket
has collected
neuron memories
that can be triggered
any second
by the latest bombs
in Ukraine…
I am in R.E.M

trapped by nightmares
that steal any sense of peace
as I collapse
under the eclipse

I can remember the pieces of another life

a pair of damp skis—

and

—the smell of cardamom *chai*

from

*nahar
lunch*

while remaining a child in hiding
(then) and—

(now) —a displaced refugee
in a country that often shouts:

*go back home!*

I will process it step-by-step
before the rumination
spirals downward.

Stop and Assess:
sense

feet touching moist earth
smooth fingers reaching for

the object before me:

my water bottle
with a wolf howling above—

pine trees sprawling at its feet, and
mountain peaks rising towards its
graceful neck.

Just breathe this scene
deep and rise upward
from the belly
to throat
to crown.

I allow myself to sink into the tub
and inhale scents of lavender.

I let epsom salt
rinse off old aches
and soothe my nerves;
for the sound of sirens
from the basement of Tehran
has been replaced by the sensation
of Tibetan singing bowls.

## The Butchering of a Child

An exorcism recording
played into the night,
and pews shifted.

I found my prayer book
underneath the bunk.

I flipped open Boy's Life
in secret while others
hummed along and
praised hymns.

I bowed my head
as we huddled
around a campfire
and roasted our sins:

wrists burst open
and scriptures spilled
screams of the possessed:

trembling we watched a
sacrificial banquet hall
waiting to prepare a child
to be crucified.

# Torn

I stopped playing with words
to make sense of the world
for the thought of being ripped

torn into tiny pieces
by a pair of scissors angling towards
my chest
as everyone watched the shredded work
made me revere the void
that I had created.

it was just a technique—
that's what the professor said:

*this is how you edit…*

And I watched his hands
as my voice trembled to the floor.

I  observed
as my belly became big
with double chocolate fudge ice-cream
dripping over a stack of fluffy buttermilk pancakes–
extra whip cream clogging my throat:

and the silent years followed:

subdued
numb…
with hamburger buns…

and the fog remained

as
I hovered
above each sentence
wondering if I would ever find my voice again.

## An Outburst from a Desperate Soul

Your ashes drift
as I grip unopened letters
to my chest—

—you wrap
your last breath
around a shroud—

I hold my tongue.

Yours decomposes.

My core remains
as I liberate the infestation
of thoughts—

*I looked like a boy.*

I was thirteen years old
when father's words—-
suffocated my embryo.

In your absence
the summer chills
kept me company.

I felt the shivers
in my throat–

so I left the symphony
and dreamt—-

—of a tiny concertina,
to catch some loyalty.

I squeezed my graces
and invoked the opaque lamp
from an antique store
and in the dim light I soothed
my misfit tears.

## Homesickness in this Stringent Atmosphere:

I wear my steampunk space suit
underneath the human skin
and step into this stringent atmosphere.

I wonder if the DNA has been decoded
as I set my heavy suitcase aside
and dream of distant planets.

I have learned that harsh moments
can be alchemized into particles of light
that unfurl from Indra's net
to help us on our ascension.

I know that I have found the way
through sitting hours on the cushion
and dreaming vivid dreams
that led me to take a vow
as I knelt with my sword.

But
I don't remember
if
I signed my Contract
with
a black
or
a blue
pen

If I ever get my memories back and
regain a sense of time,
maybe

I can recapture the comets
that I have lost along the way
as I wave to the solar system.

## A Nightingale Reaches a Crescendo

When our soil and soul began to fade
we trapped a nightingale in a cage.

I stood stained in remorse
forgetting about Farsi in the city.

You cried through protests
and blood soaked streets.

I mourned my true identity
beyond my duties
and a thousand Cypress trees—-

You served those who did not deserve
your baked hands
I rebelled against your code.

When you brought spirits
I created a chord and
freed ghazals from the tomb of Hafez—-

her songs carried our
voice into the stars.

The night sky soared.

## Sanctity of the Muses

I anoint my wrists with lavender oil
and lay my head
upon a pillow
allowing these stardust desires
and the singing bowls
to chime—
ringing in the early morning sun:

the last notes of Orpheus
please Morpheus' dreams of the night.

I awaken to a vision of infinite soundscapes—-
and welcome the notion
of a cosmic rotation:
weaving words and an ethereal voice
to illuminate geometric shapes
that whirl
beyond the constellations:

a nightingale reaches a crescendo
and I am sound again.

We can embrace this new ritual
and feel the Elysian fields
as a lyre plays in our hearts
and poetry lingers in our soul.

We can transcend the realms
and enter an eternal gate
as we gather in a celestial sphere
and sing the sanctity of the
muses.

## Plum Blossom[1]

I might have sensed your first laugh
at a lantern festival
when yellow threads of light
flickered the reflection
of a distant shore in your eyes.

I might have brushed by your shoulder
while you tamed your flute in the woods;
and in that frequency I also heard
the faint tappings of a drum
spread across a mossy rock.

It must be in this fleeting moment
that bits of our lineage crossed
as we watch snowflakes
soften underneath the moon
making space for plum blossoms to bloom.

---

[1] 梅花 (Baika) or Plum Blossom, is my Zen name. Plum blossoms appear in Japan during the winter season.

## At the Temple of Konohanasakuya-hime[2]

tyranny burrows into my bones—
the corners of my mind
wait for serenity.

I stand offering up my rakusu
as precepts blur—-
I spin inwards
losing the center of gravity—
vows almost extinct.

      *

I execute the dance of blades
melting pieces of a peacemaker
as blood disintegrates into lava.

I release my daggers
after years of betrayal
molting into a warrior.

My ancestors
who protected mountains,
climb on opposite
sides of the world
to bring me harmony—-

a snowy peak appears,
reuniting light and shadow
at the foot of Mt. Fuji.

---

[2] 木花咲耶姫 **Konohanasakuya-hime** is the goddess of Mount Fuji and all volcanoes in Japanese mythology; she is the blossom-princess, symbol of delicate earthly life.

*

In this stillness
a pacific swift takes flight
as the eternal flow lights
lanterns of my lineage:
excavating the burials of earth,
I reach beyond salty residue to
regain what I have lost—
from empty hands:

seeds of a plum blossom
and fragrance of rebirth
after the first snowfall.

## The Final Dokusan[3]
**(My Zen Teacher's Last Breath)**

I observed
as your body shriveled
and meditated in stillness—
wondering if your ashes
have kept turtles company.

After our last dokusan
when I told you about
how music had been murdered

you requested
that I keep the legacy
of the world alive

through whirling words
like a Merlin-magician
but I wasn't sure if I could
unscramble my brain
to make sense of your directions
as we approached the sesshin
at The Garrison Institute.

---

[3] 独参 (Dokusan) private meeting between Zen master and student in a room set aside for this purpose (the dokusan room).

After our last dokusan
I went for a hike
and took pictures of the amber
leaves as the sun burnt
through the camera
not knowing that it would
be the last time we spoke.

I held onto the ceramic
statue of Jizo,
found a monk's smile
to help me untangle the strings,
and emptied my hands
so that I can continue
to chop wood
and carry water.

## The Retreat

The auditorium was dimly lit
when the healer
transformed into Merlin
and transmuted the stale energy
into rays of light.

I felt intense heat
smooth over the divorce papers—
as I began to reclaim
faint tunes
of the universe once more.

I wanted to wave
my fingers mid-air
improvising over the piano keys

but the pipes were still clogged
with rancid tears—

so I let entropy reside
in my skin
as I felt bits of me slip
into the underworld.

I paused:
between each breath
as the shivers appeared again…

I huddled
beneath the bookshelves
as the selves disappeared again…

I stripped off my socks and watched toes uncurl,
on top of pebbles and the dewy grass.

I walked barefoot
through the labyrinth
and listened to butterflies
as I bathed in their flutter
at the start of a soul retrieval journey.

# The Compassion of Kami

The sacred waters of Kyoto
drip a bit of Dharma into my crown
as I bow to my katana
and sensei,
allowing kata
to sharpen my mind,
and shape me
into a peaceful warrior.

My beloved Zen teachers,
wanted me to move on
for I was low in *ki*
even though I practice reiki.

I called upon Manjushri
to help me wield wisdom
and find the way once again.

A dojo in Japan found me
through a lucid dream
and reminded me of
the Diamond Sutra,
Shinto shrines
deep bows—
the sound of the hanh
as I breathed from my soul:
pouring pure water
to cleanse my body,
and connect earth to sky.

I rise blurry eyed at dawn
and perform basic steps:
*Tai Sabaki*
and review my *shukudai,*
layering a new move
wondering if I could find my balance
in this world when my heart, the
altar
has been empty for some time.

I whisk matcha tea at dusk
and wipe my katana with *choji* oil
before bed:

a meditative practice
in this world where making contact
has become so limited.

In each fleeting moment
I perform a new kata
and imagine plum blossoms
blooming across the universe
as a harsh winter settles
into the scent of a new spring moon.

## The Dome of the Fireflies

The fairy lights of fireflies
gather in this starlit dome
and I allow myself to rest
in a clover field
that envelops the Elvish realm
and tall elder trees.

Emerald illuminates the cascading waterfalls
and a voice calls out my name:

rise:
she says,
and hands me a long sword;
this is to cut away the delusion
that you are not whole.

I rise:
a glass appears
in the kaleidoscope of time—
a little girl smiles.

Her eyes glimmer
the reflection of the moon
and fireflies glide.

Arise:
the cage you have created
is no longer a place to dwell.
The old stories leak worries that
warp your mind
and wrap around your time:
lingering in the shadows;
they are no longer yours to witness.

Fireflies flicker

their summer dance
and we are drawn
into the Northern Lights.

## Ensō: The Hand Drawn Brushstrokes

The Ensō shape is complete,
in its dance of form and emptiness
to remind us of this and that
spinning inward;
wrapping us in incense and breath.

It is the Ensō that
can encircle gritty metallic scraps
and dark chocolate
or twin flames
an ocean away
awakening when the other is asleep
but always completing
the reflection of the other.

I wonder if we can rotate
within the center of gravity,
with no duality
across time and space.

I wonder if we can embrace it all:
even when we have survived wars,
and death of those we love;
their bodies have absorbed
a mountain of clouds
and mulch insulating the soil
inside those molecules.

We can be partners in the process
as we snuggle under the covers
as our moment unfolds
as a karaoke bar plays an old-time song
and a child wonders about a supernova—
and an Ensō.

## Four Haikus

A drop of dew forms
and an empty nest remains
as the crane takes flight.

The singing bowls ring
announcing Buddha nature
a plum blossom blooms.

A night heron drinks
pure water from a blue shell
sanctity unfolds.

We sit in zazen
Enlightenment shifts in space
Cosmic chords vibrate

## Particles of Light

You wake, warm,
while I shed my threadbare skin
underneath the full moon and wait for
the red-crowned crane to take flight.

I falter through leaves
while you retreat to a mountain
and embark on your winter journey
seeking pure water in a venerable shell.

we can tip-toe
into a forgotten corner
and spin the strings of the three fates
to reveal the first snowflakes.

We can excavate the gears of gravity and
search for scraps of a dusty pendulum that
expands in an empty room
to form particles of light.

## Four Haikus

A drop of dew forms
and an empty nest remains
as the crane takes flight.

The singing bowls ring
announcing Buddha nature
a plum blossom blooms.

A night heron drinks
pure water from a blue shell
sanctity unfolds.

We sit in zazen
Enlightenment shifts in space
Cosmic chords vibrate

## Particles of Light

You wake, warm,
while I shed my threadbare skin
underneath the full moon and wait for
the red-crowned crane to take flight.

I falter through leaves
while you retreat to a mountain
and embark on your winter journey
seeking pure water in a venerable shell.

we can tip-toe
into a forgotten corner
and spin the strings of the three fates
to reveal the first snowflakes.

We can excavate the gears of gravity and
search for scraps of a dusty pendulum that
expands in an empty room
to form particles of light.

## Pods

I sit on a black cushion
and wonder
if the electric pulses
are lightbody healers
transmuting energy
through the crevices
we have created
with our breaths
to make us whole.

I rest on a pillow
and imagine
if the infinite impulses
are silver starseed-pods
traveling through the spaces
we have scattered
with our monkey mind
to make us live again.

## Amidst the Grip of Abandonment and Comfort

I awakened from resting in child's pose
I couldn't digest

silence any longer.

The beige couch
was stained heavy with sighs
that had become
the only sound of comfort
when the world had shut down.

I followed a trail of online experiences
as Cyberspace
became an infinite web of longing
and belonging:

tiny blinking orbs
began to illuminate cords
of Indra's net
as the veil between dimensions
continues to become thin
and transparent.

Through the internet
I internalized some of that blaze
to disperse the Small me
and expanded towards
the Amalfi coast of Italy
and the Northern lights of Iceland.

The orbs summoned me
to collect shards
as the tarot spread
brought forth the tower
and swept will-o'-the-wisp
out of the chat box.
I return
to lights from the city stores,
and the hum of copy machines
throughout the globe.

## A Sacred Dance

Twirling in a tattered tribal scarf
and an empty room,
I remember the empress flame
that lit the embers of an old Sufi heart.

I dream of a womb
where the ashes of a wounded bird
do not spoil.

Perhaps
it has been abandoned in a crypt
hidden beyond cypress trees
and tigerlilies to serve
me now.

Reserve these shimmies
and protect lost goddess shakes
through
maddening masquerades
in this sacred dance of stillness and shifting space

## The Lion's Gate

It's time to resurrect my light
so that I can rewire a new path
as I rewind these neuron memories
and liberate
the yellow-green speckles
from the bloated fish,
that washed up on the beach years ago.

Even if I enter the Lion's gate
the amber tapestry painted
across the August beams
still might embrace the salty residue
that trapped me in a loop for years.

The sunflowers
can circle around the smiling sun
as the illusions begin to fade from my heart.

The veil between the dimensions is thin
ever since I began to believe
and I have waited so long
for the mind to awaken
to the way
so that the magician is more than a
mere silhouette in the moonrise.

I close my eyes and bask in the orbs
that appear in the golden hall
allowing myself to chant
the spell-casting secrets from within.

I unleash my shield and reforge my sword
to spark an inner flame
to prepare me for the portal
as Leo and Sirion align with Orion's belt.

## The Lost Tribe

i never knew that
the name Osei-Afrifa
was one of royalty;
until a classmate whispered:
*you are of noble blood*—

but i had been beaten
and belittled by so many
that i didn't believe
in my own myth.

For years

i slept wide awake
until i felt stars of Anansi
and listened to
the *djembe* drum:

I danced
in the astral realm
and asked the Ashanti ancestors
to create kente cloth
so I could be clad in a regal robe.

I asked the elders
to create a ritual ceremony
as I cleared the battle fields.

I soared
above prairies
and sought safaris
that could purify
spears and swords.

I learned the ancient Akindra symbols
and sought wisdom
that would to be sewn into my cells,
as I reclaimed my name: *Nana Aqua*
and the golden stool.

## Krishna's Cart

Through the glass
of the convenient store
I watched the shriveled
hot dogs rotate
as their butchered
parts
stared
at mine and—

—I knew that
a saativic meal
could satisfy my soul
and appease the gods atop
the Majestic Mountains,
before the climb.

Kundalini had been coiled
at the base of the spine
waiting to rise

so I offered many chants
to balance the chakras–

*charkh,*
the wheel
had suddenly
become my fate;

Lord Krishna offered
a cart

to stir the embers
of my belly
with each morsel

potato samosas with sweet peas,
and carom seeds,

ginger
blended
with ghee,
to awaken a Warrior Stance

mudras
Breath of fire
Agni,

and to feel the universe
within each morsel
from Krishna's Cart.

## The Lighthouse

Let's climb the spiraling stairs
and follow the sneaky seagulls' footprints
as the sun spreads its saffron strings
beyond the ionized air
to bring our souls in tune.

Let's revel in an oceanic cleanse
and observe the widening trail
as the whirling surf kite wings
beyond the boardwalk
to nourish our relationship.

I want us to spin the sky
with salty kisses and gather up
the sand from the dunes before
to summon the sea-horse shaped branch
and the memories of floating bellies.

I want us to become breathless
with echoes of conches left behind
the scattered seashells
to awaken the rhythm of poetic drumming
and cast tubular clouds away from the tides.

We can witness the wind
waving at the shrunken sailboats,
as we swirl upwards:
the dim light leads us through
180 stairs.

We can ascend the isolation
swaying atop the mist
as we emerge on this new path:
absorbing beacon orbs
of the lighthouse.

## The Phoenicia Moon

It must have been
the constellations that illuminated
our shadow-selves
as we watched
a pink Libra Moon scoop up
the scent of rose water.

We sank—

beneath stars:
before the spring buds;
and icy roads.

The lavender salt illustrated
our velvet threads
as we surrendered
tubular clouds behind
the majestic mountains.

We embrace—

I release my collapses
and the eclipse of a winter wind
as a bear crosses the river.

You sway on top of our loft
and dance with the chimes
as a shooting star expands across the sky.

The Phoenicia moon
resurrected a sacred ritual
and the night became ours to orbit.

## Surrender

I want to see serenity
in our eyes as we explore
our souls
so that I don't have to retreat
when the amber leaves fall…

the Eastward wind is swift
lifting up the hems of a purple
bohemian skirt and
I remembered all the losses
the stairs and
the smell of death—
I collapse to the floor for
those neuron memories trail off…

I clutch the beige ruffle carpet
and watch the paisley designs
play across cloudy eyes.

I want to continue to expand
into the wilderness
and hike through
Buttermilk Falls:

see the rattlesnake shed
its skin underneath the
bare branches
as the elders around us
undress time releasing the
whiskey breath
into the ether,
and the torn tent
can slip out of my heart.

Let's exhale into this moment
since the wedding bells
were wiped off of the palms
of my hand
with fresh henna:
and surrender our storms
as we drum in unison on the fallen trunk.

## Winter Clothes

It's time to bury my winter clothes
even if ghosts layered
above my chest
still carry the November chills
that linger in the pockets
of my summer solstice shorts.

Even if I forget the retro bathing suit,
the red and black cherries painted
across my belly,
still embraces the memory of the sun
 that helped me float
for the first time.

The cotton webs and mildew
can rearrange regrets in my drawers—
as the corduroy pants loosen around my waist.

The thick fog has been severe
ever since I lost my luster
but I have waited so long
for the violet trails to awaken
my true nature
and wash archaic tears beneath
notes of a sacred waterfall.

I caress and untether my nerves
underneath my Samurai t-shirts
allowing echoes of chaos to become faint
as I unleash the dance of the blades
to banish the banshees from within.

I close my eyes and connect to the ginkgo trees
that appear in ethereal visions:
the new roots absolve invasive species
that feed on intrusive thoughts.

I shimmer and glide across the graveyard
wearing a honeysuckle-padded dress so that
my lustrous robe can shed extra pounds; as I
wrap myself around the rotating planets.

## Spellcaster

I cleared the ashes atop the altar
and decluttered my fairy garden
to grow,
for the flicker was hidden
and the words were dim
as I began to awaken:

beneath the crescent cloth
underneath the shards

I left the circle
and let the poking pitchfork
splash spurts of blue and purple
to the renewal of my heart.

I closed my eyes and let the tears drip
and dreamt of the quartz crystals to
pour,
for the light of Earendil appeared
and the planets smiled
as I began to widen:

beyond the shadows
beyond the bitter wind.

I bottled up all the yarrow in mason jars
along with stardust dreams
to dispel will-o'-the wisp
and let the moon's glow
soften the ripples
with the mating call of the fireflies,
shimmering across the water.

## Star Being

Serene beings nestle
alongside scattered entities;
tiny seeds plucked from stars,
their cells speckled with morsels of dust
that shimmer and caress us when night terrors
and old wounds drip brain saliva on to-do lists
and daily meeting notes.

A gentle wind beckons us
when clocks unwind
Underneath the canopy of a willow tree.
A tearing through time releases
toxic thoughts and limiting beliefs
that have binded our feet to
brick buildings and brunches.

Sentient beings exhale
thin slices of moon into the cosmos
and breaths that sheathe sunlight around our tender hearts.
Some might see them as lanterns among matter that
cascade in and out from where ripples form; retrieving a
rare moment of mermaids playing in the sand, long before
our original face was born.

## A Star Being's Chronicle

I thought about this book
as I was floating
on the surface of a bubble–
human etiquette for a new world.

By the way,
there are so many concepts,
besides why a bride
never gets to relax,
that I don't understand:
the imbalance of power,
brutality of war,
destruction of our planet,
and
why humans settle
for a life that isn't truly theirs.

I decided to write my book to help humanity:
*A Star Being's Chronicle*
I hope you get past the importance of hydration
and skip the advice on first dates,
and flip the pages to this section:
how to measure your mission;
when soul,
the main engine of your domain,
has crashed.

My own began years ago,
when the doors of a Zendo,
led to a Dojo:
all that bowing, breathing and blocking
beckoned me to activate my DNA,
and work with the lightbody healer,
to serenade my cells,*
and travel through the dimensions.

I thought wishing on stars was silliness
but manifestation is not a sham…
those ideas sometimes disappear
into the atmosphere—
but a few are captured by comets,
sent to the meteorologists
and dispatched through bursts of sunbeams
that pour through our pores.

I also have these enchanted map cards
that are quite handy
as I loop back and forth through space and time,
reliving harsh moments that get triggered by the
mere scent of laundry detergent.

When your life reboots your plans—
shift out of your comfort zone,
sift through the time-lines of your life,
lift your body to the skylights,
as you shed lesser forms.

I know that this office-desk-thing
was not your ideal career—
you wanted to swim with dolphins
and decipher their alien language
or become an anthropologist
and travel to New Zealand
to study the Maori culture,
instead you are feeling confined
and itchy in your human suit…

You can borrow my steampunk space suit
and see if it fits—
maybe the titanium seeds
can reveal the right chemical reaction
to free your true nature
so you can dance with your photons[4]
in the Coast of Papua New Guinea
and smile at the yellow lipped sea krait.

---

[4] credit to Chenée Fournier, an energy intuitive, medium and healer, for her phrases "serenade your cells" and "dance with your photons."

## Sorry that My Earthquake was so Profound

I wait for your clutter to fade away
so I can dispose delusions
and find the center of gravity.

The wilted flowers
welcome me into their folds
when mud became thick.

Our devotion is thinning
but we can pretend it's honey
among the broken combs.

When my mouth was shut with staples
they begin to feed my ears
with the idea of dirty diapers.

They wanted my calling
to be a silent housewife
and *forget* about my revolution.

I made bird feeders
and waited amidst ruins
to feel the stillness—

all those nights tinkering with words,
I cleared and unclogged my throat.

## We've Brought Apocalypse Through the Walls

Boxed in a cubicle
  I   paced our   dissent—
as the streets of London, Tehran
  and New York
cracked the boys choir—

      in that crevice

  your absence waxed

and the moon claimed my
 damnation.

  In our momentary lapse
you're
     pulled away

from the coast.

I
   slipped into minds of prisoners

felt jolts —

—and threw my balm against the barricade.

The piano's silhouette hides the barrier—
spilling Tori's keys, Laura's lyrics and Azam's voice

—dissolving empty pillowcases and soiled sheets.

  I release our cord     erase wedding bells

    –and cleanse this space from our insanity.

## Mosaics of the Warrior Spirit

I didn't want to live a life of craft:
  the pins were itchy and the swords needed names–
so I was reassigned to become a shield maiden
   as November brought long nights
and turkeys were cut graciously.

I wanted to see those glacier ice caves
 but the separation—

began as two snowflakes hovering above a field
 brought a silent winter-wind.

I felt the licks, warmth and eyes of the wolf–
and the legacy of a surreal canvas
awakening in my cells
when grief crawled out of me –

The hills are empty of sleds–
*you fled life.*

The clock chimes us out
 and I carry the sheathe–
no longer voiceless in my volcanic rants.

## When whales Carry our Destiny

In my winter confinement
I call the herds
as the hail storm in my heart
begins to subside.

Beyond the Caspian Sea
a whale breaches:
and in that frequency,
I hear the wails of a mother.

I remove sweat off of marked barstools
where patriarchy plays
and behind the stage—

–I watch and wait
as water spills my tears
into a gallery.

Before our expiration date
I dreamt of scenarios:

faces that form
my tribe:

a large pond reflects
unity–
the dead and alive
Vows of a legacy–

and

a statue of a woman
riding a horse that has heard
the cries of *Vatan:*

*My homeland.*

## A conversation with Sophia's Universe

I navigate this world,
kneading dough for company
as I swirl about memories
like tea
in a delicate chipped cup–

I move through the stars
spheres rotate between seconds
and I whisper to crystals when you are gone:
for the closets were just emptied of camping gear–

and when I sleep through the sleet and snow
the umbilical cord is released
before I rush into my own ravine.

Cosmic scissors unchain me:

I scribble secrets within the sacred box
and wait for cherubs to rush before me,
fluttering scents amongst the ripening seeds

## The Taboo of the Hand

The camp counselor split
our sex in half
so semen
could be saved:

beneath the cloth of God
we sat in chairs
to hear the word.

trapped under church bells
good boys & girls nodded
as a video spoke of our temples—

desecrated
by our obscene mind
and blasphemous touch.

Our wholesome nature
was to be preserved
beyond the flesh:

but I hadn't discovered the juice
of my body *yet*

the trace under my belly
was faint—

Now—
drawing circles around my
bushy triangle

I disrobe and wrap myself
in rose scent and settle into the tub

let water drain–

tuck myself under the fiber
and feel pieces of flesh
falling like petals
into my hand

My solitude has spoken.

## Songs of Qoqnoos

Songs rise from the ashes
as *Qoqnoos* burns away debris
of thistles and last bits of sterile soil
from the chambers of my heart.

The spring Equinox brings *Nowruz*
as I tumble through tombs
and burst from beneath the snow
like a lustrous tulip.

I recite poetry and swing on wings
of origami doves that allow my mind
to bring back memories from the wind:

I was once adorned in green bands,
beaming up the sky with love and hope
as we cheered for peace at Cafe Nadery
and beyond Washington Square Park.

I breathe into dandelion seeds
as a turquoise egg emerges
and cracks open—

*donya* wraps around us
as the phoenix burns our sorrows
so we can emerge as starseeds
bringing forth divine feminine energy.

## Generation X Marks the Spot

I wonder if the field hockey girls
have accepted my punk path
as we merge with kicks
now in harmony—

Let's build a temple to seduce Athena
so that new nutrients for my cell
can replace the scorched slot.

that's where my darkness
drifted into flames that brought
back my breath—

I strayed
to untangle vines from my hips—

and let go of scraps of dirty green
as a black belt fills in the void
when I touch a palm
amidst lingering pain.

I feel a life-line infusing my heart

for

our generation allowed cloudbusting
to submerge into the subconscious

and

voices spin me as
we split our atoms within the fluidity
of this space.

the   grunge   girl
leaves her glass coffin.

## A Warrior's Heart

It seems foolish to pretend that my heart
can wait out these little tugs and bites.
For years I let the shadows play
and invisible fears inflame my flesh.

I waited to be fierce
but
beneath the climb
I stumble,
between words
I stutter.

When the light flickers,
knives glint
and
tricksters play.

I drink:
the sweet warrior blood bestowed upon my ancestors
and their swords that never fled in the heat of the battle:
to rip through my melancholic cocoon.

I crave this sweet aphrodisiac to take root.

# Publications

I thank the publications in which these poems first appeared:

"The Basement of Tehran" in **International Human Rights Arts Festival**, December, 2022 forthcoming in **IRANIAN WOMEN SPEAK** anthology, 2023

"The Butchering of a Child" forthcoming in **Ghost City Press**, 2023

"An Outburst from a Desperate Soul" forthcoming in **Journal of Expressive Writing**, 2023

"Torn," in **The Seedling**," **The Seedling Poetry**, 2022

"Homesickness"/ retitled as "Homesickness in this Stringent Atmosphere" in **Grey Sparrow: Issie 41**, January, 2023

"A Nightingale Reaches a Crescendo" in **Journal of Expressive Writing**, November 14, 2022

"Sanctity of the Muses" **Calliope**, 2022

"At The Temple of Konohanasakuya-hime" forthcoming, **Indefinite Space** 2023

"Plum Blossom" in **Braided Way**, March 25, 2022

"The Final Dokusan"/"My Zen Teacher's Last Breath" in **The Seedling Poetry**, 2022

"The Retreat" in **Literary Heist**, September 20, 2022

"Kata"/"Compassion of the Kami" in **Clinch** 2022

"Dome of the Fireflies" in **Quail Bell**, September 16 2022

"Enso" known as "The Hand Drawn Brushstrokes" in *Amethyst Review*, 2022

"Three Haikus" in **Amethyst Review**, 2022)

"Haiku" in **Quail Bell** in 2022 September 16, 2022

"Particles of Light" in **Cacti Fur** July 6 2022

"Pods" Cacti Fur, July 6 2022

"Blinking Orbs"/ "Amidst the Grip of Abandonment & Comfort" in **The Seedling**, 2022

"A Sacred Dance, 2021, by **Active Muse**.

"A Sacred Dance," 2021, in **Active Muse** also published by **Soul Lit**, 2021

"The Lost Tribe," podcast, **Deep Overstock**: Issue 18 October 1, 2022

"The Lion's Gate," podcast, **Deep Overstock, Issue 18**, Issue 1 2022

"The Lost Tribe" & The Lion's Gate" in **Deep Overstock Old Favorites**, Issue 18 anthology, October, 2022

"Krishna's Cart" **Fresh Words**, 2022
"The Lighthouse" forthcoming **Calliope**, 2023
"The Phoenicia Moon," in **Quail Bell**, September 16, 2022
"Surrender," in **The Academy of the Heart and Mind**, June 7, 2022
"Winter Clothes" Forthcoming, **Calliope** 2023
"Spell-caster" in **The Opiate**, July 23, 2022
"A Star Being" in **Star*Lit**, 2022
"A Star Being's Chronicle" in **Bethlehem Writers Roundtable**, Autumn, 2022)
"We've Brought the Apocalypse Through the Walls," forthcoming, **Clockwise Cat**, 2023
"Songs of Qoqnoos" forthcoming, **International Human Rights Arts Festival, IRANIAN WOMEN SPEAK**, 2023
"A Conversation with Sophia's Universe,"  reprinted with the permission of **Burningword Literary Journal** and the author.
"A Warrior's Heart" in **Soul-Lit**, 2021

# Acknowledgments

I wish to thank Kurt Lovelace and Michael Sofranko for their support and encouragement to publish this collection. Without them this book would have not existed beyond my imagination.

I thank my editors, John Compton and Ken Valenti, who helped me throughout the process of this publication.

I also thank the following people for their continued support: Judie Eisenberg, for her mentorship & clarity to take a different journey with my writing. Chenee Fournier, for being my life coach, intuitive guide, and helping me overcome my fear and believing in me more than I could have ever done myself. Charity Helton, who created a fantastic website, and an amazing travel companion. **The Creative Breath & For the Love of Words** Writing Groups, for allowing for a sacred space to share my work. Shiva J Layer, for accompanying me to Iranian art shows in NYC & helping me improve and translate my Farsi. Fariborz Khandani & Shirin Khandani for their continued familial support, advice and encouragement. Raquel Navarro & Chandni Rodriguez for their incredible in depth yoga classes in which they teach with soul and heart. Cindy Terp for always making me feel like a part of her family and Penny Thieme for her continued mentorship, sense of community & for giving me my first featured reading experience with **VALA Gallery**. I would also like to thank the staff at **White Plains Public Library** for their continued support.

My heartfelt gratitude to all of the various Zen & martial arts instructors that I have worked with over the years, spanning from Japan to New York. My training has continued to help me cultivate my focus and balance.

I extend my gratitude to my Spirit Guides and my ancestors, who I honor each day by living with courage and being the peace I wish to see in this world.

Finally, I thank my mother, Parivash Khandani for supporting me in my chosen path after years of sacrifice.

**Caroline Reddy**

# Caroline Reddy

Caroline Reddy was born in Shiraz, Iran to an Iranian mother and a Ghanaian father. She spent the first eight years of her life in Tehran, Iran before locating to Paris, France, and finally settled with her family in Westchester, New York. Caroline Reddy is a Reiki master, a Zen practitioner and a student of taekwondo. Her work has appeared in numerous journals including ***Active Muse***, ***Calliope***, ***Clinch***, ***Ghost City Press***, ***Grey Sparrow***, ***International Human Rights Arts Festival***, ***Star\*Line*** and ***Tupelo Quarterly Review***, among others. In the fall of 2021, her poem *"A Sacred Dance"* was nominated for the **BEST OF THE NET** prize by ***Active Muse***.

Caroline Reddy lives in New Rochelle, New York. For more information please visit https://www.carolinereddy.com.

www.ingramcontent.com/pod-product-compliance
Lightning Source LLC
Chambersburg PA
CBHW060544080526
44586CB00012B/856